WAITING FOR THE STORM

Gerald Mangan was born in 1951 in Glasgow, where he worked as a medical artist after leaving university. He has since lived as a poet, painter, illustrator and literary journalist in various parts of Scotland, France and Ireland, and has reviewed poetry and fiction for some years in *The Scotman* and the *Times Literary Supplement*.

During the mid-1970s he worked as an actor and playwright at Theatre Workshop in Edinburgh, and later as writer-in-residence at Dundee College of Art and at Deans Community School, Livingston. He was awarded writer's bursaries by the Scottish Arts Council in 1978 and 1986. *Waiting for the Storm* (Bloodaxe Books, 1990) is his first book of poems.

GERALD MANGAN

WAITING FOR THE STORM

BLOODAXE BOOKS

Copyright © Gerald Mangan 1990

ISBN: 1 85224 110 1

First published 1990 by
Bloodaxe Books Ltd,
P.O. Box 1SN,
Newcastle upon Tyne NE99 1SN.

Bloodaxe Books Ltd acknowledges
the financial assistance of Northern Arts.

LEGAL NOTICE
All rights reserved. No part of this book may be
reproduced, stored in a retrieval system, or
transmitted in any form, or by any means, electronic,
mechanical, photocopying, recording or otherwise,
without prior written permission from Bloodaxe Books Ltd.

Requests to publish work from this book
must be sent to Bloodaxe Books Ltd.

Typesetting by EMS Phototypesetting, Berwick upon Tweed.

Printed in Great Britain by
Bell & Bain Limited, Glasgow, Scotland.

Acknowledgements

My thanks are due to the editors of *Aquarius*, *Bananas*, *Cencrastus*, *Cracked Looking-Glass*, *Cyphers*, *Gallimaufry*, *Glasgow Herald*, *Honest Ulsterman*, *Literary Review*, *New Edinburgh Review*, *Poetry and Audience*, *The Scotsman*, *Seer*, *Times Literary Supplement* and *Verse*, where most of these poems, or earlier versions of them, were first published. Some have also appeared in the anthologies *Green River Review: New British Poetry* (University of Michigan, USA), *The New Edinburgh Review Anthology* (Polygon Books, 1982), *Beyond the Shore: Irish Writers in Exile* (Northampton, 1985), *Five Writers in Residence* (Dundee College of Art, 1987) and *Poetry with an Edge* (Bloodaxe Books, 1988); and several have been broadcast on BBC Radio Scotland, BBC Radio 4, *Poetry Now* (BBC Radio 3) *Poet's Choice* (Radio Telefís Eireann) and the series *In Verse* (Scottish Television).

Particular thanks and acknowledgements are due to the Scottish Arts Council, for the assistance provided by a Writer's Bursary and a Writing Fellowship.

Contents

9	Glasgow 1956
10	Ailsa Craig
11	Death of an Islandman
12	Concerto for Television
13	Bad News, Long Awaited
14	Glasgow, Underground
15	New City Road
16	Jonah in Partick
19	The Recluse
20	Heraclitus at Glasgow Cross
22	Kirkintilloch Revisited
24	Gunfight at the Govan Corral
26	Last
27	Nights in Black Valley
28	Prometheus Unemployed
30	Snow
31	Double Bed
32	Composition
34	Gulliver in Dublin
36	The Midland Scot
38	Aberdeen
39	A Trial Separation
40	A Class on Yeats
41	Edinburgh
42	A Road in Fife
44	Night Wind at Ramornie Farm
45	Birch Bark
46	Wood Axe
47	Wasp Nest
48	Waking up in America
49	Freeway
50	Scotland from 30,000 Feet
51	Schopenhauer in Leith
52	Two Coastlines
54	God
56	Four Seasons
58	Deadlines
59	The Laird of Ardluggan
60	Scotland the Ghost
62	The Early Flight
63	Waiting for the Storm
64	Leaving Dieppe

Glasgow 1956

There's always a headscarf stooped
into a pram, nodding in time
with a plastic rattle, outside a shop
advertising a sale of wallpaper.

There's a queue facing another queue
like chessmen across the street;
a hearse standing at a petrol-pump
as the chauffeur tests the tyres,

the undertaker brushes ash off
his morning paper, and my mother,
looking down at me looking up,
is telling me not to point.

The background is a level site
where we recreate the war.
Calder Street is Calder Street,
level as far as the Clyde.

Without a tree to denote it,
the season is moot. That faint
thunder is the Cathcart tram,
and the sky is white as a trousseau

posed against blackened bricks.
A grey posy in her hands,
the bride stands smiling there
for decades, waiting for the click.

Ailsa Craig

It bulked large above my sandcastles:
a stepping-stone from a land of giants,
with a noose of surf around its neck.

One blustery sunset, turning purple,
it reared above my father's head
as he slammed outdoors from a row,

to sulk on the fuming causeway.
Geysers of spume were spouting high
as he strode down past the warning-signs,

and the last light was a hellish red
as he dwindled, stooping, into the rocks,
and drowned in my streaming eyes.

He'll be right back, my mother said.
But I saw the Irish Sea overwhelm
a rage that could shake a tenement.

He'd never looked so small, and wrong.
I never knew what drove him there,
but I saw him thrashed by a stormy God,

and he never seemed so tall again.
I'd never seen him so whole, before
I saw that tombstone over his head.

Death of an Islandman

1

A skirl of pipes. The wind squeals
through the reeds as he winds
the gramophone-handle, and the wax draws
the needle to the end of the reel.

Idling on the quilt, his fingers
have forgotten the scales, the stops,
the crust of salt on the creels.
His sails are reefed, and he forgets the knots.

Docked in a high tenement,
where the light-bulb hangs by a hair,
he listens to the cistern fill,
and hears the tide at the harbour wall.

2

The sand in the sand-glass doesn't flow,
and the bottleneck is Glasgow.
Blue above a thicket of stacks,
the hills to the west have drawn away

like the water from Tantalus,
and the branch that never bends
down to his thirst. A slow air,
that flows away in his sleep.

The needle hisses, and the record spins
like water draining in the sink.
He listens to the sounds of closing-time,
the bottles breaking in the street.

Concerto for Television

The first violin is bowing low.
In close-up, with the sound turned down,
his *scherzo* is a show of thrusts
and parries with a fencing-foil.

The conductor has conjured up
the storm with a wave of his wand:
the tic in his nervous cheek
gives away the turmoil.

As the flautists simper coyly,
and the cellists saw at their knees,
the tubists turn to fish-eyed
gargoyles, slick with oil,

and the chorus turns the silent
pages back to silence.
The kettle-drummer raises steam
and simmers to the boil,

but the harpist with the limbs of willow
is picking flowers from the wood.
Bending in the wind, she plucks
a bunch of notes out, clear of soil.

Bad News, Long Awaited

Sift through it for something else.
Opening a sack as flaccid
as a belly after birth, the postman
has snapped, with the letter-box,
the tightrope I could hardly walk.
And whatever I'm doing now
becomes the net: raking out ashes,
say, or putting a breakfast back.

What I'm feeling is something else.
Looking both ways at the lights,
not weeping, I'm giving one ear
to what I'm thinking: *'It happened
just as I thought...'* I forget
the tension in the line I'd taken,
and what follows, now the line's gone slack.

It's not so much the news itself:
it's hearing the story arrange itself.
*He was a ghost, thereafter, of his former self;
and when the bush of roses
at the window pricked his eye,
he could hardly even bleed. But instead
of haunting himself, he began to pack.*

Glasgow, Underground

The conductor at the dead man's handle,
rolling from side to side, is trying
to roll a cigarette between the stops.
He licks his fingers to make it stick,
but the carriage rolling from side to side
makes the sliding door slide open,
and the draught blows the shreds apart.
He shuts the door, but the stop comes round,

so he stands up from the dead man's handle,
rolling his eyes to heaven, and yells
Cowcaddens! and sticks it in the tin.
When he opens the door, the carriage empties
and fills back up from the other side,
and his hand fills up with tickets and coins
that make his fingers slip. He shuts the door
as the train starts up, and opens the tin,

and licks his fingers at the dead man's handle,
and the paper sticks; but the door sliding open
blows out the match. He shakes the box,
and his face falls like wax on a candle,
and he rolls his eyes in a circle of hell.
Something tells him the stone he's rolling
up this hill will roll back down.
Cowcaddens! he shouts, and then *Hell.*

New City Road

> *La forme d'une ville change plus vite, helas!*
> *que le coeur d'un mortel.*
> BAUDELAIRE

The ball swings, and the walls collapse,
and a cloud of stone-dust haunts the gap.
   The city walls were built to last.
   The city walls are falling fast.

The floors cave in. The ceilings flap
like flesh around an open heart.
   We're tearing down the fire-traps.
   We're tearing up the city's maps.

Up from the basements, roofless rats
quit the scuttled ship in packs.
   The city's hold is filling fast.
   The city spires are sinking masts.

We've looked so long, our eyes are black
hearths in a gable, staring back.
   My birthplace is a verge of grass.
   My father's grave is an underpass.

My tongue is ringed by stumps and gaps.
On the roof of my mouth, the plaster cracks.
   Here comes the wrecker, to wreck the last.
   Here comes the future, to raze the past.

Jonah in Partick

1

The waters have compassed me about
summer and winter, down here in the dark.
Lying low in a basement, looking up
at a tenement due to come down,
I weigh the storeys astride my head,
and count the years since the rain began.
It's an endless hiss against the glass;
and the layers of sandstone round the bed,
sunk in clay as deep as the Clyde,
are shipping it through open gills.
It stains the walls, this seeping damp.
It musts my clothes, and softens my bones.
How long now till it wears out the stone,
this water that's compassed me about?

2

The billows and waves pass over me.
I feel them pound beyond the wall,
and move in time. My ears are clams,
but I hear the bells clang out the hours,
from a kirk-spire sunk in the sea-mud.
Rolling and swelling, the peals rise up
like flotsam through the fathoms,
into the innards where the light's failed.
Is the whale I inhabit white outside?
It's not absorbing light. And it spouts
and wails in its rage all night,
like something close to death. *Yahooryi...!*
Like something close to birth, I feel
the billows and waves pass over me.

3
The weeds are wrapped about my head.
In the half-light, under a ceiling of ice,
jade-green fronds and sea-fan tresses
flow in my face from a shelving floor,
and press up flat, just short of air.
That creaking membrane never parts
to let the sun look more than a bubble
trapped on the underside. But this is the light
I see by best now. I know where I am,
when I'm feeling my way. Born in the dark
by the sign of the fish and the water-bearer,
I'm used to the weight. It holds me in place.
Ice-bound, waterlogged, I flourish here
like the weeds wrapped about my head.

4
I go down to the bottoms of the mountains,
till there's nothing I'm not below:
the ruckle in the stank, the dripping rone,
the mop-pail clanking in the stair-well.
Under black umbrellas, turtle faces,
pale underbellies, legs treading water,
I go down through circles, with a roaring in my ears,
and shake with the tremors of the Underground.
It sends out waves, and I give back an echo
from the pit to the blind gut:
Does a single circle of tunnel and track
mean nothing but nothing? Cramped in my shell,
at least I know all ways lead up
from here, at the bottoms of the mountains.

5

Out of the belly of hell, I cry:
out of my skull, with my eyes of ice.
Out of the foghorn mouth of the Clyde,
that opened up wide and swallowed me.
Out of a city docked in its past –
a rusted hull, with a cargo of smoke.
Out of the walls I was born inside,
whose openings all lead into dark.
Out of the woman who led me below –
who opened her lips and wrapped me up
in silence, under a quilt of snow.
Out of the waters that break and deliver me
out to the light, that vomit me dry
out of the belly of hell, I cry.

6

The earth, with its bars, is about me forever.
Propped by the elbow on oak, making
circles of hell from circles of beer,
I drink the poison of standing waters.
I curdle the milk of paradise.
It's the white sky, and the black street:
they make so much of grey, you'd never know
heaven and hell were a hair's breadth apart.
Crossing the bar, I open my eyes
at the mouth of the close; and all it takes
is a moment of sunlight thrown off the water,
to hear the tree, with the hidden nest
praising it out of the depths:
The earth, with its bars, is about us forever.

The Recluse

What is it in the sunlight
of the afternoon, breaking
through the leaves at the window,
that throws me out of true?
As the wind moves the tree
and the tree moves the light,
the light makes the wall
a turbulence of bubbles
shoaling out of the deep,
and brings me to a standstill,
questioning the floor.

I'm waiting for the kettle,
and the news. That's all.
What's buried down below,
that acts like air
enclosed for years, behind
the port-holes of a wreck?
A fist of bones,
creeping up and gripping
my heart without a sound,
is shaking something loose.

What is it in the light
that makes the silence spread
like a stain of water,
and makes me fall
down through it, all at once?
I fall through storeys
of dead air, mystified,
till waves of salt wash me up
in darkness, in something
like innocence down there.

Heraclitus at Glasgow Cross

Where Gallowgate meets London Road
    and the world walks out with his wife,
umbrellas sail in long flotillas
    through streets you can't cross twice.

The old home town looks just the same
    when you step down off the Sixty-Three.
The jukebox music takes you back
    to the green, green grass of Polmadie.

Everything swarms and eddies in smirr.
    Wine flows out from the Saracen's Head.
Mascara runs, like soot from a guttering.
    Day-glo signs glow green on red.

Something for Everyone. Nothing for Nothing.
    Social Security Estimates Free.
It's Scotland's Friendliest Market-Place.
    Watch Your Handbags, Ladies, Please.

Watch the Do-nuts fry in grease,
    the tailgate-auctioneers compete
with the broken-winded squeezebox player,
    wheezing through his leaking pleats.

Or under Clyde Street's railway arches,
    see the stubbled dossers soak
like debris snagged in shallows, blowing
    old Virginia up in smoke.

Down where the fishwives trade in rags,
    they curl like snails in paper shells:
lips of sponge, skins of mould,
    eyes like cinders doused in hell.

They're watching concrete fill the docks,
    the bollards rust on the graving-quays.
The green green grass grows overhead,
    on gantries still as gallows-trees.

Where Gorbals faces Broomielaw,
   the river's black and still as ice.
When the ferryman takes the fare, he says
   You can cross this river twice.

Kirkintilloch Revisited

Crying to God, 'I fear Thee no longer'
As the blackbird does, for a few fine days.
                    DANTE, Purgatory

1

Turning their backs on the sabbath,
the miners stamp a circle
of asphalt hard on the towpath,
and pitch up coins in the snow.

The slag-heap they threw up here
is levelled to a sports-pitch.
The pit-head is rusting
like a nail in Scotland's waist,

and the church ringing for mass
rises like a new leviathan
out of the shale. It spouts
new liturgies for a new estate,

but the sabbath is as it was.
The pub is a locked pillbox,
ringed with barbs, and the gamblers
swig from a wrapped bottle.

2

This ridge between the foothills
and Glasgow was the rampart
where Rome drew the line,
between history and snow.

The white of the Fells
out-stared the legions,
and the empire's wall is rubble.
But the stones are in the name –

a church on a fort on a hill,
where Rome came back as a dove
and gripped like winter.
Above the sandstone school,

where they taught us Pliny and the litany
and tawsed me for disbelief,
the cross on the spire is black
as a cassock against the snow.

3

The church disgorging
a mass into the car-park
clangs its tongue at the blackbird,
for reading the season wrong

and singing, out of turn:
I fear Thy wrath no longer.
A feather of white breath
flutters at every mouth,

and a raucous synod of crows,
holding court in the tree-tops,
is taking him to task.
But he sticks to his theme:

the thaw on the Forth-and-Clyde
as it winds around the foundry,
and the crocuses open-mouthed,
like nests of fledglings.

Gunfight at the Govan Corral

Leather-skinned from the desert heat,
Jingling spurs on stirruped feet,
A stranger rides down Calder Street.

Weathered stetson pulled down low,
He's six days' ride from Mexico.
The tram-lines make the going slow.

Tall and gaunt and saddle-weary,
Caked in dust from the endless prairie,
He's got his sights on Gordon Carey –

The rattlesnake from Gorbals Cross,
Who stole his sweetheart, Senga Ross.
If he bites the dust, it's no one's loss.

From the high sierras of Maryhill,
Through tumbleweed in Provanmill,
He's trailed him; now he'll shoot to kill.

Colt Forty-Fives slung low on his hips,
A smoking lolly between his lips,
He's reining up for a bag of chips.

Blue eyes crinkled against the glare,
He's tethering his thirsty mare
When a gunshot shatters the brooding air.

Dust spurts up, beside his boot:
Carey's missed him by a foot.
He dives for the Co-op door, and shoots.

Come out, he yells, *and show some pride,
You yellow skunk. You stole the bride
of the fastest gun in Kelvinside.*

Facing his doom with tight-set jaws,
As the clock strikes, and a buzzard caws,
The villain snarls a curse, and draws.

A blink of the eye is all it takes
To miss the move the stranger makes.
Slick and smooth as the tongue of a snake,

His muzzle spits a deadly flame.
The bullet bearing Carey's name
Finds its mark, and ends his game.

The hero blows his nails, and strolls
Home for his tea. The credits roll.
The sun sets over the Govan Toll.

Last

Hardly a face now that doesn't hold
every brick of the city
in the balance of its eye,

or spell out, syllable
by syllable, everything
the landscape leaves unsaid.

Raised at the vanishing-
point of the wake, the wave
a dockhand gives on the quay

sinks like a voice
on the brink of sleep:
the leaden motion

of a parting gesture,
already perfect
before it evolves.

Nights in Black Valley

Hours when nothing but the rumours
of the mountain fill your ears:
the vixen wailing, or the whisper of rain
as a cloud caresses the roof.

Hours when nothing moves in the house
but the spider and its thread,
the candle spilling its tallow
when the draught disturbs it,

or the grubs worming from the log,
shrivelling into the flame.
The eye of the dog is entranced,
and his shadow is a behemoth.

In the morning when the light breaks up
the conspiracy of mists,
and the flock flows down to the water
like a liquid finding its level,

the time comes round to choose
what to leave and what to take
back to the electricity.
And I memorise the silence:

the moon sliding on the lough,
as the stars endure their space.
And the hawk stropping his beak,
like an axe dreaming of wood.

Prometheus Unemployed

1

Tapping my knuckles in time
to the swing of my foot,

and the watch scratching in my ear
like fingernails on a drumhead,

I keep time to kill the time
that's hanging heavy on my hands.

At the limit of the pendulum,
I'm as still as the fulcrum.

2

The clouds I blow out
are my souvenirs of fire,

like the tongue of ash in the grate.
Like the burns along the table-edge,

the coins I count from the jar
are so many links in the chain.

Listen to the clinking,
as they run through my hands.

3

In the cavern under my ribs,
my thoughts coil and hiss:

famished serpents, making
a meal of their tails.

When words are all you eat,
the syllables swell like bubbles

and eclipse the sun, before
they burst on the tip of the tongue.

4

My flesh will blend in time
with the rock at my back;

but the speck overhead,
plunging out of the sun,

is focussed on my navel
like a burning-glass.

When its beak gets to work,
it's wearing my face.

5

Idle hands have peeled my layers,
onion-like, to the final tear;

and all the circles have exposed
is why the circles were enclosed.

I've seen enough of what's inside.
It's what the skin's designed to hide.

Come devil, or come devil's men.
Put my surface back again.

Snow

That wind from Mizen Head,
whimpering round the walls
like a dog day and night,
was a kind of ultimatum.

Gorse burned on the cliff,
but the taps coughed ice.
Chopping driftwood to lift
the mercury up to the mark,

I was sparring with shadows,
and biting my tongue:
chopping logic, till
the dark was white.

Circling the point
without sharpening it,
I'd drawn the night
to the end of its tether

when dawn came up
like an envoy with a pardon,
and the ceiling glowed
with a borrowed light.

The whiteness prised
my lids apart.
Whiteness eclipsed
the idea of white.

Double Bed

1

When day broke and dovetailed
the sky into the chimneys,
the mirror framed the street,
whose windows mirrored ours.

The room was all right angles,
but your body proved them wrong:
like the rain falling aslant,
that made the uprights oblique.

You made the corners curves.
Like the spout of the kettle
sprouting a flower of steam,
you softened the naked light.

2

When the last note of the clock
fell like a ripe apple,
you held it in your mouth.
You tuned your voice to mine,

and held my face in yours;
and your body broke my falls
like a wave accepting rain.
I heard the sea in your heart,

and fell like a willing Icarus.
How often did your surface break
before I saw my falling image,
rising upward from the bed?

Composition

> *It is said that Fra Filippo was much addicted to the pleasures of sense...if he could by no means accomplish his wishes, he would then depict the object which had attracted his attention, and endeavour by discoursing and reasoning with himself to diminish the violence of his inclinations.*
>
> VASARI

1

You lie back only
   till your backbone sickens,
then you fidget the pose.
   You squirm around
on a ticklish buttock,
   or getting goose-pimples,
burst into sneezes.
   This is how it goes
with a subject not an object.
   Keep still, life, still:
pretend you're an apple.
   Repose. Repose.

2

You can't relax? But it's you
   should be coaxing me –
whose private parts
   are the real exhibit;
whose soul is on show
   at the end of the brush,
and who never knows
   if the work will work.
Keep still. Keep still.
   It's bad enough
that the draught dishevels
   each page I touch.

3

And the shape you are,
   it's harder still:
these undulations,
   globes and hollows —
all so *whole*,
   till my eye dissects you
limb by limb,
   and I lay you out
so bare, so cool,
   on a slab of white.
Lie still, lie still,
   till I sharpen my tools.

4

Moving, you tempt
   my touch all the more.
Make me flinch
   from the glare of white,
and I'll drop the brush.
   I'll let it stiffen,
and reach, if you will,
   into that dark, that bush
that makes me weak, and make
   you move, and move,
till we both lie still.
   Till your touch cloys,
and coiled in your thighs,
   I itch for the brush.

Gulliver in Dublin

1

Waking on the strand, with sand in my ears
   and sewage washing my head,
I found my limbs and body bound
   by a thousand lengths of thread:

woven with all of a spider's skill,
   in monkish knots and coils –
too fine to hold me down for long,
   too intricate to spoil.

How many years had I overslept,
   when I stirred, and made them cower?
The last I knew, I'd nodded off
   over *The Will to Power*,

and the next I knew was the whispering
   of the Union of Catholic Mothers,
as a thousand tiny needles
   stitched my flies together.

Leopold Bloom went through my pockets,
   and rolled away a copper.
The Archbishop marched across my chest,
   to shrink me with holy water.

As he blessed my stubble in Gaelic
   and flicked his aspergillum,
I stood up for *The Soldier's Song*.
   And the rest is all on film.

2

I learned to be more circumspect
   here, where nobody grows
taller than the tinkling steeples,
   or the flags at Lansdowne Road.

Where the rows of rooftop aerials
   spread out like beds of nails,
and God, in the lap of his mother,
   conforms to the local scale.

Where voices are never raised above
   the foghorns on the quay,
and the ships tied up at the Custom House
   turn their backs on the sea.

Where even the hills are tied down fast,
   like tarpaulins over hay,
with a mesh of dykes and boreens
   to stop them blowing away.

I had to stoop very low, to hear
   the gossip in Grogan's Bar:
It's all in the poor lad's head. He's read
   too many books, by far.

It was then that I took that mouthful
   out of the Galtee Hills,
and spitting it into the ocean,
   retired to Hy Brasil.

The Midland Scot
(Holyhead to Glasgow)

1

Stirring tea in a plastic cup,
caught up in the eddies
around the spoon, I've missed
the gist of what the guard,

bustling north at Crewe,
has drawled above the small-talk
and the clicking of the points.
The voices rise with the sun,

but the vowels are flat
as the snow on the allotments,
and England is a muttering
as bland as the tea.

A curdled land of milk
and sugar wrapped in paper.
A country for counting
potting-sheds like sheep.

2

Numb from the night crossing
and chafing the blood back,
I can't stop embarking
from Irish ground.

I breathe a mist of whiskey
in a rising sea of hills,
but I'm frozen in a gap
the current can't jump.

When the neck of a swan
in a ditch catches
my eye like a fish-hook,
it's a question-mark:

I'm fumbling for a match
down the back of the seat.
I'm stretching a gap
time will close up.

3

The poles file past,
roped together at the neck.
The sleepers roll up
like a rope-ladder at my back.

The branch-lines of thought,
at a tangent to the eye,
have petered out in sidings
and abandoned conjunctions

when the Rs of a stationmaster,
rolling *Carstairs*, connect
like cog-teeth. They move me
all the way back, repeating

There's no point of no return,
till all the lines converge,
and the vast rictus of Central
opens over the Clyde.

Aberdeen

A grey slick of gulls on the swell.
The smell of fish and whisky
hanging like spindrift,
and a spark of frost in the stone,

where the stone rebuffs the sea:
proof against all the fustian
the sea throws in its face.
It won't stand for fancy stuff,

and won't give an inch
to the wind, or the chisel.
It knows its mind so well,
it hardly needs to speak it:

standing sound as ever,
in a dream of ice and brimstone.
It's the sea, without the oil,
that ground its edge like this.

A Trial Separation

Something suspended in the air
afterwards – as if my last word,
stretched out by the silence
like elastic from my mouth,
was set to snap back
in my face;
           or a train,
gone off the rails, had inched
its weight down a bank, and teetered
out from a precipice – only just
held there by a coupling.

Something in the absence
I handle like a presence:
as if I were moulding you
from the air with my gestures,
like a mime leaning his weight
on a figment;
           or after rain,
a tree just declined to drip,
and hoarded all
the downpour it caught –
a niggard with a windfall,
its palms held up.

A Class on Yeats
(Livingston New Town)

I walk through the schoolroom unravelling
his long-knitted thought, word by word,
as a pupil loosens her plaited hair,
to look for split ends. The strands
flow round her head until
she sticks at a knot, and it loses shape.

I move my hand to show the feints
of the swallow through his thought,
and watch his riddles cloud their eyes.
Who can tell the swallow from its flight?
I'm waving in air, to clear a mist:
paring the myths, to lay him bare.

Here below the strip-lights,
where concrete chokes the echoes,
we pluck the feathers from the swan
till the facts cast off their shadows.
The gilt flakes from the nightingale,
and Cuchullain's loading an Armalite.

On the road home by the sausage-works,
where the slaughterhouse vans unload,
that livid red between the ribs
never looks so raw, and dead,
as when we've picked him to the heart,
as though the artist were the art.

Edinburgh

Bound in lambswool, tweed and foxfur,
skin as pale as her antimacassar,
my landlady sits on the edge of her seat
to announce a rise in the rent.

The east wind tousles her drying-green,
but everything indoors is in place.
The wallpaper is a regiment of roses,
marching round a newly-crowned Queen.

She picks a scone from a tartan tin,
and nibbles. '*Everything is going up.
It's regrettable...*' And her lips impart
a lobster kiss to the bone-china cup.

She learned this poise with a book on her head,
but it's capital that keeps it high.
Her bank's no castle in the air,
but a church grounded in rock.

The keys of my house are in her purse,
and the law's on her side of the case.
Cushioned on her couch, without an ashtray,
all I can see is my lengthening ash.

A Road in Fife

1

My short-cut into town
runs level through the howe
for a mile, without a bend.

It's the width of three lorries,
and long enough to wonder
if history has gone to earth

forever, somewhere down
in the miles of abandoned faces –
the workings under my feet.

2

It runs past the open-cast mine,
where bulldozers shift the earth
to quarry sand now. Day after day,

they pile it up for the sifting-machine,
that dumps it into the tip-up trucks.
As the pile rises, the pile goes down.

*Lifting dirt to put it back down
drives you daft*, a driver says.
But this is the only work in town.

3

It comes to a point in a hollow
where the village clusters round
the shell of a distillery,

a church for cut-price carpets,
and a column with a poppy-wreath.
Walking there and back, all winter,

I note the queue at the video-shop.
I hear the choir in the Masonic Halls
rehearsing *Keep Right On.*

4

Is it the dwarf-oaks leaning
away from the wind,
where warrens starve the roots –

or the car-wrecks dumped
at the crossroads, where
the crows talk down from the wires?

Or is something amiss in my life,
that this is just a map of,
waiting to be read?

5

It takes me back to the dream
where you run in sand, forever,
and the earth turns in time with you:

where spring keeps backing away,
and death is catching you up.
When I look back over my shoulder,

I'm staring back from where I started –
sitting with my father on an empty street,
in a van that refuses to start.

Night Wind at Ramornie Farm

It picks on our weak points:
rattling the hinges
and the rusted guttering,
till you'd swear the house
was straining like a tent,

and the tree at the gable,
flailing and clawing,
nags me like a tooth.
Just sleep, you said.
It sounds worse than it is...

But that's what keeps me up.
The wind might be bluster,
but the branches pick up
every hint of menace
like a bundle of nerves,

and blow it out of scale.
They roar like a shaman
tormented by omens,
as if they were reading
what the wind has written:

as if they gave a curse
for the echoes inside,
and the flaws in our fabric –
the tensions under the roof,
that make my axe-hand itch.

Birch Bark

> *Living things in contact with the air must
> acquire a cuticle, and it is not urged against
> cuticles that they are not hearts.*
> SANTAYANA

An hour of dusting surfaces
with the vacuum whining,
of scraping the dog's hair
in tufts out of the rug,

and the day forms a skin,
like milk cooling. Whatever
was forming in the liquid
has sunk out of reach,

and even the sea lets me down
when I climb the hill with the sun.
I look beyond the surf,
and surface is all it shows –

till the dog writhing
his moult off, succumbing
to grass and rapture,
starts to crack the glaze;

and the tractor dragging
a comb up the slope,
opening a furrow
to a cloud of gulls,

shows me the earth
evolving into light.
I remember the heart
depends on skin

as the sea on air,
and the flaking bark
of the birch is bringing
word out from under it.

Wood Axe

Carved willow,
curved for the hand
and balanced like a fiddle,
the shaft is kin
to the logs on the block
that wound its neck:
the marbled elm,
the hard-hearted apple,
the chicken-flesh of ash.

It's the head that's deadly:
swooping down like this,
clean through the grain,
its edge invented
the first straight line.
Dividing and multiplying,
segmenting the circle,
it's the head that turns
the forest into numbers.

Wasp Nest

That seething globe, gummed to the loft-beams,
swelled all summer like a tumour.
They chewed our logs to pulp for it –
ploughed gouges out of the doors.

My torch-beam showed a crusty moon,
a spew of whorls like cyclones.
Gorged on juice at raspberry-time,
it bloated like a puffball.

Smoke and spray-cans couldn't stop
the buzzing in our ears – the swarm
sinking its stings in our dreams.
It outgrew both our heads

and festered into autumn,
till they stumbled home like drunks.
When frost grounded the last of them,
I listened hard to its silence,

and cut it down. Sawed in half,
a loaded womb came to light:
a birth-passage, winding up
through a sump of dry corpses

to the packed decks of larvae,
counting down to spring.
The fumes from the bonfire
were incense, clearing the air.

Waking up in America

1

I'm still in flight with the dawn at my back
when I touch down on mohair, barefoot,
and leave you curled in your summer chemise.
These tidemarks on my shoes were snow,

but the white at the window is Pacific mist,
and the toothpaste grin of the Pontiac
is California. Smoking from a soft-pack,
hearing an anthem in the humming vents,

I descend into time. It's seven a.m. by KGO.
The news is brought to me by the makers
of Holenut Crackles, Compliments of Nature,

and the shower-faucet has swum into my ken.
Sleep on, wife, and dream something new:
this world was yours when I discovered you.

2

I've been for a walk, with my back to Europe –
down Ninth and Lighthouse, to Ocean View.
I followed the cliff-path out to the point
where the waves roll in from Asia,

and nothing's ever made me feel so small
as the falcon, hanging fire in the blue.
Its circles chilled me like Ishmael's
crow's-nest hymns to the whale.

I've come to earth now, breathing scent
from the steaming leaves of the cypress;
but I've brought you back my vertigo.

Wake up, my love. The sun's caught us up.
We've followed history west, and now
I'm just as giddy on the precipice.

Freeway

1

The pedal's flush with the floor.
The verge between the exits
is an unbroken graph,
and the moon's neck and neck.

Set your stakes on this baize,
and there's no doubling back.
Headlights and tail-lights
are corpuscles in a vein.

But the motion's all as still
as your eye in its mobile
continuum: rolling on the spot,
like a ball below a weir.

2

Each glint consumes the last.
The impact of insects,
or your ash blowing back
as you wind down the window:

it's all over as you blink.
Nothing blurs, or lasts.
As the snake eats its tail,
and dawn swallows the moon,

we eat up the miles,
abreast of our shadow:
longing for a turning,
as the eye craves its lid.

Scotland from 30,000 Feet

Cruising south from the Ice Age,
with an ice-cream indigestion,
I see a hunchback toppling westward,
chasing a kite with a tail
of ribbons into the sea.

Why do I think of Kierkegaard
suddenly, leaping into the dark?
Ankle-deep in the moonlight,
with a lacing of snow on its hump
and the hills rolled up to its knees,

it's frozen at the point of take-off:
pinned to there and now,
at the hollow of its belly,
by a million yellow
needle-points of light.

Schopenhauer in Leith

The mist off the firth
making nothing out
of nothing, makes
the whistle of the fishmonger,
slicing off heads,
stop me at the open
doorway of the shop.

His lips pursed
in a circle and the knife
in perfect tune,
running up and down
the scales, cut clean
through flesh and bone –

clean as a gem.
Let this be all
the world I need
make word for now:
each note a facet,
cutting a perfect
circle in the mist.

Two Coastlines

East

is a cool diagonal, pointing
straight to the oil and the ice –
a carriageway, where we enter
all the distances in the log;

where the book-keeper leans like a sundial
over his figures, measuring
the day with his shadow, counting
each minute as a wedge of pie;

and the sun is a canny lawyer,
seeking loopholes, drying up fogs –
a stickler for shades of light,
who'll split the hairs on a fly,

and portion all the premises
as nicely as the proofs.
Flush with stone, the stone
is a face too hard to embellish –

too clean for a weed
to take a hold. Free of dust,
the past is under glass.
We handle only what we need

for the counting of profit and loss
the keeping of law and order,
the chopping of chapter and verse,
the tilling of soil and sea.

West

waves and curls like wrack, like locks,
forward and back; a line that winds
or ravels in knots, and never wants
to know how far it's travelled.

Where the wind's a drunken whistler
colliding with the wind; and the tides,
colliding in the sound,
tear up the timetables.

Where rain shuts the distance out,
and bracken buries the track;
where the mist muffles the sun
and the moss muffles the rock,

and the plough describes a circle
round the mystery of a circle –
a stone as fast in earth
as a false god in truth.

Weaving and twining like foam, like ivy,
over and under, the line invents
its own turnings, and its own end
returns to its own beginnings:

a broken fort and the memory of siege,
a rusted sword and the memory of shining,
an empty chalice and the memory of sacrament,
a cornered voice and the memory of singing.

God

1

In the beginning was a cloud
without a beginning:

like the smoke above Govanhill.
Swallowing the notion

gorged and dizzied me,
like a bellyful of candy-floss.

2

His flesh was ashen,
and soggy on my tongue;

but he lashed us from the pulpit,
through wine-red lips.

He saw through the crust of hair-cream,
to the stained silk of the soul.

3

Towering above my father,
snipping my back and sides,

he read me across my shoulder.
His shadow stood in my light,

till the summer I saw the light
beyond the stains in the glass.

4

That tissue of sins
I whispered through the screen

fell apart like my old blazer,
when I pedalled into the hills.

Every time I stretched,
it split along the seams.

5

In the end he was a word
stripped of its capital:

a brain-child of the fire
that banished the dragons.

He was a cloud behind my father's eyes,
like smoke trapped in a cave.

Four Seasons

1

When the sun rises from the wheat,
the mist rises with it. When you sit
up from the pillow, your hair falls
all the way down to the sheet.

When the wind rises, it makes
a wave in the wheat. You show me how,
when you brush out your hair:
how a wave flows, and how it breaks.

2

When the smoke rises from the leaves,
the leaves rise with it. The dead wood
catches, and the fire throws
our shadows up into the trees.

When your hand opens, you show me
the leaf you take from the air.
In the dead veins, you make me see
a living image of the tree.

3
When the light rises from the snow,
you rise with it. Your eyes,
opening like petals, fly
in the face of the white below.

When a flake falls on your brow,
you glow with it. You never saw
a city as white as this city,
and you make it all new for me now.

4
When the sap rises in the wood,
the river rises with it. You take me
up to the tree-line, to listen
to the mountain in full flood.

When the dark falls, you remind me
how a fire burns into silence,
how dead wood flows downhill.
And you make me listen for the sea.

Deadlines

1

In the cold hour when the window turns
from coffee-black to ashtray-grey,
all he sees is the page turning black.
And he envies Crusoe his lack of ink.

2

The hours surge like sleepwalkers
towards a closing departure-gate,
as he packs and unpacks his luggage:
treading the air, against the current.

3

How many notes has that blackbird sung
in the century since his last full-stop?
How many snowflakes fall on the roof
as he shakes a verb, like a matchbox?

4

His lids weigh more than his bookshelves,
but the rest of him is liquid paper.
As he curls on the couch, like a comma,
his life is a paragraph, half-erased.

5

He envies the snow, which has no editor;
and his dreams fall into its shapes.
He restores the white between the margins.
He dictates an Arctic of silence.

The Laird of Ardluggan
(Tune: The Laird of Cockpen)

The Laird of Ardluggan, he's proud and he's broke:
The estate and its state of affairs is a joke.
The affluent days of Ardluggan are past;
But he's keeping appearances up, to the last.

The house of Ardluggan's a moribund heap:
There's bats in the corbels and rats in the keep.
There's rot in the rafters and worm in the floor.
There's worm in the sheep and a wolf at the door.

The shrubbery's wild, the vermin are tame,
The mouse and the maggot make free with the game.
The roads are subsiding. The drive needs a Hoover.
The Range Rover doesn't have room for manoeuvre;

But down at the jetty the forty-foot yacht
Gives a wide berth to the resident rot.
Incredulous creditors watch him decamp
Every year to the Med, where he creeps from the damp.

The Laird of Ardluggan he's proud and he's broke.
His sporran is light, but his tailor's bespoke.
The affluent days, he admits, may be gone;
But he's keeping the cutlery out of the pawn.

His back to the fireplace, roasting his kilt,
He's playing the patriarch up to the hilt:
Paying the piper to play the strathspeys
With whisky in crystal, and elegant praise.

His voice is a resonant bass without treble –
All Gordonstoun plums, and Balliol pebbles.
He's Scotch to the core as a rack of old malts
Distilled in St James, and matured in the vaults.

His heart's in the Highlands, at bay with the stags,
But pickled in spirits, his eyes are in bags
As he weeps in the goblet, remembering Flodden –
Forgetting what side he was on at Culloden.

Ardluggan, Ardluggan, you're proud and you're doomed.
The clouds in the gloaming are gathering gloom.
Go saddle your stallion, dress up in your best,
And galloping gallantly, sink in the west.

Scotland the Ghost
(Tune: any bagpipe music)

It's no deid, the auld land, it's no deid in spirit:
All it wants is a stirrup-cup, and a coronach to stir it.
Drinking up at closing-time, it's girning in its chains:
O when, O floo'er o Scotland, will we see your like again?

It's no deid in spirit, no, it's never done with haunting;
But it never makes its mind up, to tell us what it's wanting.
The spirit's weak without the flesh, but still it lifts the hackles –
With its head below its arm-pit, and its ankle still in shackles.

It drags the sword of Wallace, it's lugging Bruce's helmet;
But spiders make their webs in it, and a draught would overwhelm it.
The heart inside the armour's like the queen inside her cell:
The breath of Knox has chilled it, and blasted it to hell.

The crown fell off with Jamie, when he took the English tiller;
The head fell off with Saltoun, who sold the tongue for siller.
When Bonnie Charlie dreamed his dream, to stick it back together,
He met a butcher's cleaver, and it ended up in slivers.

The heart grew black as Glasgow, then, and rumbled underground;
The disembodied head was known as Edinburgh town.
When Burns sprang up to sing of flesh, and earth, and barley-grain,
He sang too low, too late to touch the Socratean brain.

Sheriff Walter found the body stripped to bare essentials,
And shivering in the heather; but he saw its true potential.
He dressed it up in tartan plaid and kilt, for exhibition,
Installed it in his stately home, and charged them all admission.

Victoria had it dance a fling, and played it for a puppet –
A gillie on a string, without a *sgian dubh* to cut it.
Mass-produced in clockwork, it made the perfect vassal
To paint the atlas red for her, or dandle in her castle.

Burke and Hare worked double-time, supplying all the clients
Who analysed the body in the interests of science.
Doctor Jekyll knew the head was severed from the heart,
And drank a heady potion to explore the private parts.

MacDiarmid woke in a whisky haze, and saw a headless thistle –
Stuck his own on the prickly stalk, and sharpened up the bristles.
He kept the spirit neat and drank it deeply through a chanter,
Till the skull swelled beneath the skin, and stretched his Tam
    o'Shanter.

It's no deid, the auld land, it's no deid in spirit:
All it wants is a drunk man, and a World Cup to stir it.
In Gallowgate, in Canongate, it's girning in its pain.
It's watering the stones to make the floo'er bloom again.

The Early Flight

Among the naked shelves,
and the pale rectangles
where the pictures soaked up smoke,

I'm awake before the blackbird:
brushing my teeth in a mirror
that's glad to see the back of me.

Why am I padding around
like a burglar now,
as I check the emptied drawers?

The ghosts are still out cold.
And they won't come round, until
I've left them under a cloud.

Now that I've edited
my life down to a suitcase,
like a small work of art,

it's the present I'm remembering.
Rinsing out the coffee cup.
Packing the ticking clock.

Waiting for the Storm

It's the sweeper with the torpid broom
wading through swamp-air, mopping his nape;
the mounds of crayfish waving feelers,
clawing space, and craving sea.

The dogs announce it, and the tingling comb.
It's the flash on the overhead Métro,
the beaded cleavage advertising
fan-cooled booths, for quick relief.

It oozes out from a bed of glaur,
till crooked fissures open in the cloud –
a jagged hand, on airmail blue.
It's the welling up that blurs the page,

and the deluge wipes it clean:
the window slamming suddenly inward,
and the clatter of running heels,
like a burst of automatic-fire.

Leaving Dieppe

The white ship hums. The deckhands in oilskins
coil up the last of the line,
and the bluster of the Channel on the front
shakes me awake. Beyond the breakwaters,
in the first light, I cross the threshold
where France becomes your face.

As the gulls fall back, and the heaving deck
acts out the turmoil of leaving,
I hold on hard, at the stern-rail,
to that last wave you gave:
the way it fell, as the guard whistled,
and you pressed a kiss to the glass.

Ta langue m'a entrée, my love:
your tongue is still on my lips.
What do I gain by this translation
through water, into a cold horizon?
The prow dissolved in spume
is your breast in its froth of lace,

and every thought's a feather's weight.
Thrown from wave to wave, through
bottomless troughs, they leave me
nothing to declare but this.
Not a word seems worth your touch,
or calms me, like your calm embrace.